LIFESKILLS™

HANDBOOKS

Moving Out
on Your Own

Nan Bostick

and

Susan M. Freese

21st CENTURY

SADDLEBACK
EDUCATIONAL PUBLISHING

ISBN-13: 978-1-61651-660-4
ISBN-10: 1-61651-660-7
eBook: 978-1-61247-348-2

Printed in Guangzhou, China
1111/CA21101811

16 15 14 13 12   1 2 3 4 5

Contents

Section 1	**Preparing for Independence**	5
Chapter 1	Knowledge and Skills Checklists	8
Chapter 2	Attitude Assessment	14
Chapter 3	Budgeting Time	20
Chapter 4	Budgeting Money	26
Section 2	**Finding an Apartment**	33
Chapter 1	A Housing Checklist	36
Chapter 2	Comparing Classified Rental Ads	42
Chapter 3	Filling Out a Rental Application	48
Chapter 4	Rules for Roommates	54
Section 3	**Moving In and Getting Settled**	61
Chapter 1	Change of Address Forms	64
Chapter 2	Ordering Phone, Utilities, and Internet Service	70
Chapter 3	Buying Essential Household Goods	76
Chapter 4	Renting a Moving Truck	82
Section 4	**Solving Common Problems**	89
Chapter 1	Do's and Don'ts for Tenants	92
Chapter 2	Unexpected Expenses: Revising Your Budget	98
Chapter 3	Revising Rules for Roommates	104
Chapter 4	Tenants' Legal Rights	110
Word List		116
Index		118

Preparing for Independence

Turning 18 makes someone an adult in the legal sense. But being an adult involves much more than age. Adults have the knowledge and skills to live on their own. Adults also make their own decisions and accept responsibility for what they decide—no matter what the consequences. Can you do these things? Are you ready to be an independent adult?

It Takes More Than "Planning"

Derek had never been a "morning person." Throughout high school, he struggled to get to school on time. Many mornings, he slept right through his alarm. Then his dad would try to wake him. It usually took Dad three or four trips into Derek's room before Derek actually got out of bed.

By the fourth trip, Dad was mad. "You're 18 years old!" he would remind Derek. "You need to start acting like an adult!"

Derek already thought of himself as an adult. After all, he'd just graduated from high school. And in the fall, he planned on going to the community college. He hadn't talked to anyone at the college yet about being admitted. But he was pretty sure he'd be able to get in.

This summer, Derek was working full time doing landscaping. He had to be at the worksite at 7:00 a.m. Most days, he managed to get up on time. His co-worker Jack picked him up. Derek knew that if he wasn't ready, Jack would leave without him.

Next month, Derek planned on moving into a house with Jack and a few other guys from work. He'd been spending a lot of time there, and he looked forward to moving in. He just needed to save enough money for his share of the rent and utilities.

Derek was making good money at his landscaping job. And he loved that his employer paid him in cash. He didn't even need to have a checking account! But he always seemed to run out of money before his next payday. He thought about asking his dad to help out with the rent.

Chapter 1

Knowledge and Skills Checklists

Most young people are eager to become independent adults. But what does it take to make it on your own in today's world?

One way to judge your **readiness** is to **inventory** your **competencies.** What's the current level of your knowledge and skills? What additional knowledge do you need? What basic skills require more development?

Readiness
Being prepared and willing to do something.

Inventory
To list or record.

Competencies
Skills and abilities.

Complete the following checklists to help you see how far you've come—and how far you need to go—along the path to successful adulthood.

General Knowledge and Skills

Review the following list of ***essential*** knowledge and skills. For each item, rate your ability level — from 1 to 5. Be honest!

Essential
Necessary or required.

I do this . . .				
Not so well			**Very well**	
1	2	3	4	5

I've developed the ability to . . .

_____ 1. balance my wants and needs.

_____ 2. work hard for what I want.

_____ 3. manage my money.

_____ 4. express myself clearly.

_____ 5. make wise decisions.

_____ 6. resist peer pressure.

_____ 7. respond to emergencies.

_____ 8. cooperate with others.

_____ 9. manage my time.

_____ 10. solve everyday problems.

Tips for Handling Peer Pressure

- Choose friends who influence you in positive ways. True friends will respect your values and decisions.

- Think in advance about what a specific situation might involve. Avoid people, places, and activities that involve things you don't want to do.

- Make decisions that fit your values, not other people's values. And then stick with your decisions, no matter what others do.

- Consider the possible consequences of your behavior: Could you get in trouble? Could you get hurt or harm your health?

- Practice ways of saying "no." Either tell the truth or make up an excuse, but be able to tell other people "no."

SAY NO TO DRUGS!

Specific Knowledge and Skills

Review the following list of specific knowledge and skills. For each item, identify your competency by writing Y for "Yes" or N for "No."

I know how to . . .

_____ 1. take care of my health.

_____ 2. cook simple dishes.

_____ 3. write a résumé.

_____ 4. manage a checking account.

_____ 5. dress properly for different occasions.

_____ 6. investigate job opportunities.

_____ 7. use the library and Internet to find information.

_____ 8. prepare for a job interview.

_____ 9. create and stick to a budget.

_____ 10. schedule an appointment.

_____ 11. make simple home repairs.

_____ 12. use public transportation.

_____ 13. write a business letter.

_____ 14. fill out forms properly.

_____ 15. get information from maps, charts, and graphs.

_____ 16. get legal help.

_____ 17. understand and follow directions.

_____ 18. take care of my clothes.

_____ 19. apply for a driver's license.

_____ 20. register to vote.

Work on Your Social Skills

Social skills are the behaviors that help people get along and communicate well with others. Key social skills include the following:

- Being polite and friendly
- Controlling anger
- Resolving conflicts
- Apologizing and accepting responsibility
- Compromising (not having to get your own way)

Having good social skills will help you be successful in everything you do. Social skills are important with your peers, with your family, and at your job.

To develop your social skills, work on these things:

- Knowing what to say and when to say it
- Listening effectively to others
- Understanding body language and unspoken signals
- Knowing how to behave in different situations

Chapter 2

Attitude Assessment

Suppose you've developed the necessary knowledge and skills to go out on your own. Good for you! Now it's time to check out your attitudes.

What are your basic values and beliefs about yourself, others, and the world around you? Do they tend to be negative or positive?

Having a good attitude can help you through many difficulties. Overall, being positive can make your life much happier. Having a bad attitude can create serious problems and make you unhappy, as well.

Build Your Self-Confidence

Self-confident people generally have a positive attitude. They believe in themselves and their abilities. And their good attitude makes others believe in them, as well. Being self-confident helps them succeed in whatever they do, no matter how difficult. How can you build your self-confidence?

- Work hard. Do your best.
- Do what you believe is right.
- Behave honorably. Act with virtue.
- Be honest. Admit your mistakes.
- Don't brag, but accept compliments gracefully.

What You Think and How You Act

Do you realize how negative attitudes show up in your behavior? Think about the following examples:

Attitude	*Behavior*
"I'm always right."	• Blame others for your own mistakes
	• Don't accept **constructive** criticism
"If I'm not perfect, then I'm no good."	• Make excuses
	• Avoid responsibility
"Might makes right."	• Act loud and pushy
	• Won't **compromise**
"Rules are meant to be broken."	• Don't respect authority
	• Are late and argue
"The world owes me a living."	• Are lazy and slow moving
	• Expect others to provide for you
"Why try? Things never work out for me."	• Have low expectations
	• Are willing to give up

Behaviors That Hold You Back

No one is perfect. One way or another, we all tend to have some negative attitudes.

How do *you* express your negative thoughts and feelings? Be honest with yourself:

→ When you're under pressure, are you a know-it-all, a bully, or a victim?

→ Are you a perfectionist? Do you get upset if things aren't exactly the way you want them?

→ Do you overreact? Are you a hothead?

→ Do you respond slowly or even refuse to follow directions?

→ Do you give up too easily because you expect to fail?

These are only a few of the negative attitudes that limit success.

Constructive
Positive and useful or helpful.

Compromise
To reach agreement with others by giving up some of what you want.

Turning Things Around

Of course, it's easier to see bad attitudes in other people than ourselves. Think, for example, about someone who gossips all the time. Trying to make yourself look good by making others look

bad is a sign of insecurity. The gossiper may not realize that—but other people do. They know they can't trust someone who gets attention by pointing out other people's problems.

Being successful in life begins with making a good *impression* on others. So, it only makes sense to check out your attitudes. Some of them may be *immature* or downright self-defeating. If you've already realized that, then you're taking a step toward change!

Changing attitudes takes time, patience, and lots of practice. But the good news is that you can do it if you really want to.

Impression
A general idea or feeling.

Immature
Not fully developed or grown. In describing attitudes and behaviors, it can mean childish and irresponsible.

Be a Good Friend

What qualities do people value in friends?

- **Loyalty:** Support others in bad times as well as good times. Don't let a disagreement end a friendship. Don't gossip or speak badly of others.

- **Generosity:** Share what you can with others. Be kind and thoughtful.

- **Understanding:** Be a good listener. Ask questions when you don't understand someone else's opinions or beliefs.

- **Honesty:** Tell the truth. Don't lie to make someone feel better. Instead, suggest how to fix a problem.

- **Acceptance:** Show you care about others even when you disagree with them. Try to see others' points of view. Look for new ways to think about issues.

CHAPTER 3
Budgeting Time

Have you learned to **budget** your time? Successful adults are good time managers. They **schedule** their activities to make sure they won't fall behind. They remember important dates, because they plan ahead.

Budget

To plan or organize into specific amounts. The word *budget* can also be used to mean the actual plan that's made.

Schedule

To plan when one or more things will happen. The word *schedule* can also be used to mean the actual plan that's made.

Jessica's Calendar

Jessica has a hectic schedule. She goes to school every weekday, and she works part time at night and on weekends. From time to time, she has appointments. And she has regular chores to do in the apartment she shares with her roommates. In addition to all this, she has a social life.

How does Jessica keep her schedule straight? How does she remember where she has to be at any given time?

Jessica has a system for budgeting her time. She keeps track of what she needs to do by entering it on a calendar that's on her cell phone. That way, she can look at it throughout the day.

21

Setting SMART Goals

The first step in creating a good schedule is to set goals. Think about what you want and need to do in a certain time period: a day, a week, or a month. Then set goals according to this SMART plan:

S **Specific:** Make goals clear. Focus them on work, school, social activities, and chores.

M **Measurable:** Find ways to measure your progress. Doing so will help you stay committed.

A **Achievable:** Make sure you can reach your goals. Set goals based on your knowledge and skills.

R **Relevant:** Set goals that relate directly to your life. They will be easier to achieve, and you'll work harder on them.

T **Time-bound:** Set dates for completing your goals. Also set due dates for steps to complete along the way.

Here's Jessica's calendar for September:

Sunday	Monday	Tuesday	Wednesday	Thursday	Friday	Saturday
		1 class 8-12 work 1-4 study 4:30	2 class 10-2 work 4-6 gym 6:30	3 class 8-12 work 1-4	4 class 10-2 work 4-6 gym 6:30	5 chores 9-11 Sanjay 7:30
6 study	7 class 10-2 work 4-6 gym 6:30	8 class 8-12 work 1-4	9 class 10-2 work 4-6 gym 6:30	10 class 8-12 work 1-4	11 class 10-2 work 4-6 gym 6:30	12 chores 9-11 family bbq 3:00
13 study	14 class 10-2 work 4-6 gym 6:30	15 class 8-12 work 1-4 study 4:30	16 class 10-2 work 4-6 gym 6:30	17 class 8-12 work 1-4 haircut 4:30	18 class 10-2 work 4-6 gym 6:30	19 chores 9-11 Mia's wedding 7:30
20 study	21 class 10-2 work 4-6 gym 6:30	22 class 8-12 work 1-4 Alex's bday	23 class 10-2 work 4-6 gym 6:30	24 class 8-12 work 1-4 Dr. B 4:30	25 class 10-2 work 4-6 gym 6:30	26 chores 9-11 Sanjay 3:30
27 study	28 class 10-2 work 4-6 gym 6:30	29 class 8-12 work 1-4 library 4:30	30 class 10-2 work 4-6 gym 6:30			

Jessica's "To-Do" List

Jessica also creates a daily "to-do" list on her phone. Every evening, she looks at her calendar. Then, she makes a list of things she needs to take care of the next day.

Jessica sets *priorities.* She lists only those tasks that are important for that day. She doesn't include everyday tasks, such as brushing her teeth and getting dressed.

Priorities

Things of greatest importance.

Jessica goes over her to-do list throughout the day. She checks off or crosses out each item as she does it.

Here's Jessica's to-do list for October 1st:

→ 8:00–9:00: English homework

→ 9:00–9:30: Math homework

→ 10:00–2:00: Classes

→ Free time: Buy birthday card for Alex; buy wedding gift for Mia

→ 4:00–6:00: Work

→ 6:30–7:30: Gym

Wasting Time at Work

The average American worker wastes two hours every day. And almost half that time (45%) is spent surfing the Internet for personal use. Here are the top-five online time wasters:

- Checking or updating Facebook
- Looking at videos on YouTube
- Playing online games
- Shopping
- Managing profiles on social media Web sites

Setting Priorities

How can you achieve all your goals for the next day, week, or month? Learn how to set priorities:

1. Write down your goals on a piece of paper.

2. For each goal, ask yourself two questions: How important is it and how urgent is it? (In other words, how quickly does it need to get done?

3. Next, rate each goal from 1 to 4. Use a 1 or a 2 if it is something really important and has a specific deadline or time frame. Use a 3 or a 4 if it is something fairly important and can be accomplished at a later time.

   For instance, seeing a new movie that's come out might be important but not urgent. If that's the case, then give it a 3.

4. Rewrite your list of goals. Put them in order from the lowest to the highest number. The goals with the lowest numbers are your highest priorities. Find ways to achieve them when you plan your schedule."

CHAPTER 4

Budgeting Money

Living on your own forces you to
manage your money carefully.
That means making a plan for
spending. Follow five steps to
create a basic budget.

1. Figure Out What Your Income Is

Consider all your sources of income. Add up what you get paid at
your job, any gifts or allowances you receive, and the student loans
you have.

Base your earnings from your job on your actual paycheck, not your
overall wages or salary. Remember that part of your earnings will be
taken out of your paycheck and paid as taxes.

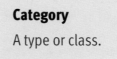

2. Decide What You Can Afford to Spend Each Month

How much can you afford to pay for rent? How much should you spend on food? What about transportation, utilities, Internet, and phone costs? You'll also need to budget for insurance, health care, clothing, and entertainment. What percentage of your income should you spend on each?

Category
A type or class.

Look at the chart on page 28, which lists some average U.S. household expenses. Look at each *category* and how much of the monthly budget goes toward it.

Looking at this chart should give you the basic idea of what's called a *balanced budget*. In a balanced budget, the total expenses equals the total income. (Note that all the percentages add up to 100%, or the total income.)

Category	Percentage of Income
Housing (rent/house payment, utilities and public services, household supplies, furnishings, etc.)	33%
Transportation (bus or train fare, car, gas, insurance, parking)	20%
Food (groceries plus eating out and "to-go" food)	15%
Personal insurance and retirement plans	11%
Health care (doctor, dentist, insurance, medicines)	7%
Personal care (products and services, such as clothing, haircuts, dry cleaning)	5%
Entertainment (movies, sporting events, concerts, music downloads)	5%
Education and reading (tuition, fees, books, materials)	2%
Miscellaneous (gifts, vacations, etc.)	2%

3. Create Your Own Budget

Use the sample chart to create your own budget. Set up your own categories, and base the amounts on *your* expenses and income. Do your budget on paper, or use a computer program or online tool.

High-Tech Tools for Budgeting

Many computer programs are available for help in creating a budget. One of the most popular is Quicken, which you can buy at a computer or office store. Other programs are available online, including Mint and Mvelopes. Many of these programs charge a fee for use.

Benefits of Using Budgeting Software

- You can set up your own categories to track your expenses.
- You can link the program to your bank account to record deposits.
- You can pay bills online.
- You can be sure all the math is done correctly.
- You can create pie charts and other graphics to review your spending.

Drawbacks of Using Budgeting Software

- It takes time and repeated use to learn them.
- There is a security risk to have your information on your computer or online.

Estimate the dollar amount for each category. You'll have more control over spending in some categories than in others. For example, you can limit the number of movies and concerts you go to. But you can't tell the electric company how much you'll pay.

Remember that some bills come only once or twice a year (such as auto insurance). But each month, you should put aside some money. That way, you'll be able to pay these bills when they're due.

4. Keep Track of What You Spend

Each time you pay for something, record it in the correct category. At the end of the month, add up what you spent in each category. Keep track of your monthly totals.

5. Adjust Your Budget to Fit Your Needs

At the end of the month, compare your spending to the amounts you budgeted. Are you on target? Is your budget balanced?

Suppose you're spending too much in one category. You have two choices: Either *adjust* your budget or spend less. If you spend too much in one category, you have to decrease spending in another category by the same amount.

Estimate
To judge or guess at the amount or value of something.

Adjust
To change or correct.

30

[FACT]

Top Money Wasters

How do you waste money? Many people overspend in these areas:

1. ATM fees
2. Lottery tickets
3. Gourmet coffee
4. Cigarettes
5. Infomercial products (such as Snuggies and Magic Bullet blender)
6. Name-brand groceries (instead of store brands)
7. Eating out
8. Unused gym memberships

Saving Money on Groceries

- Use coupons.
- Buy store-brand products.
- Make foods on your own, instead of buying them ready made.
- Buy in large quantities at a warehouse or low-cost food store.
- Plan meals around items on sale at the store.
- Plan meals a week or two ahead, and buy only what you need to fix them.
- Keep a grocery list posted in the kitchen, and add items as you run out of them.
- Grow your own vegetables.

Finding an Apartment

Most people will tell you that getting their first apartment was exciting! They might not tell you, though, about the difficulty they had finding and renting that apartment. And they might not admit to the troubles they had getting along with roommates. You can avoid all these problems by learning some guidelines for finding, renting, and sharing an apartment.

Making the Right Move

Gia and Griffin are thrilled! The 20-year-old twins are ready to move out on their own. And they've decided to look for an apartment together.

Both have good daytime jobs at the department store in the local mall. They started working there in high school. Over time, their part-time jobs turned into full-time positions. At night, the twins take classes at the nearby community college. Gia is in the fashion design program, and Griffin is studying business.

The two have been talking about getting an apartment for some time now. And they've worked hard to put together a monthly budget. They plan on sharing expenses such as utilities, groceries,

and transportation. And both will have to reduce spending somewhat on entertainment—at least for a while. Together, the twins figure they can afford a monthly rent of $900.

Gia and Griffin have never looked for apartments before. They aren't quite sure where to start. Their mother suggested they look in the local newspaper. The "want ads" section contains listings of available apartments. A friend told them they could find the same kinds of listings online at Web sites such as Craigslist. And an instructor at the college told them to drive around the neighborhood just outside campus. Many of the homes in the area have apartments for rent. Signs saying "Apartment available" are sometimes posted in the yards.

Some of the twins' friends think they're crazy for wanting to be roommates. In a way, though, Gia and Griffin have been roommates all their lives. They know each other quite well. And over the years, they've learned how to settle their disagreements. They're sure they can make this work!

CHAPTER **1**

A Housing Checklist

If you wanted to rent an apartment, what things would you look for?
What questions would you ask the apartment manager? What would
you want to know about the neighborhood? And how would you
compare the ***pros and cons*** of different apartments?

Determine Your "Needs" and "Wants"

A good way to start looking into apartments is to brainstorm a list of features. Get a paper and pencil, and list all the things that come to mind. If you'll be sharing the apartment with roommates, involve all of them in this brainstorming activity.

Next, think about which items on your list are "needs" versus "wants." What features *must* the apartment have? And what features would you *like* it to have?

One basic need is how much you want to spend for rent. Another important need is the number of

bedrooms and perhaps even bathrooms. Likewise, when you want to move in is important. In general, your needs are specific and not adjustable.

Your wants will probably not be as important in choosing an apartment. For instance, you may want to have an apartment with a swimming pool. But you could go without, if you found an apartment that had other more important features.

Pros and cons

Positive and negative points or qualities. Benefits and drawbacks.

Make a Checklist

Take your list of features and create a checklist, like the one that follows. Include key details at the top, such as the apartment address and contact information. Also include features that you consider necessary near the top.

Related information should follow—for example, costs such as utilities. Also make note of the terms of renting, such as the requirements of the *lease.* Finally, features that are truly wants should go near the end.

APARTMENT CHECKLIST

Apartment address: _____

Manager: _____ Phone number: _____

Number of bedrooms: _____ Number of bathrooms: _____ Date available: _____

Costs/Terms

Monthly rent: $ _____ Deposit required: $ _____

Utilities included: ☐ None   ☐ Electricity   ☐ Heat

  ☐ Water/Sewer   ☐ Garbage/Recycling   ☐ Other:

Terms of lease _____ Move-in specials? _____

Location

☐ Safe neighborhood?   ☐ Noisy street?

☐ Grocery store nearby?   ☐ Bus stop nearby?

How far from work? _____ How far from school? _____

Features

☐ Clean?   ☐ Bathtub in bathroom?

☐ Building security?   ☐ Manager/Caretaker on site?

☐ Major appliances furnished?   ☐ Air conditioned?

☐ Enough closet space?   ☐ Additional storage area?

☐ Garage or carport?   ☐ Off-street parking?

☐ Swimming pool?   ☐ Workout room?

☐ Party room?   ☐ Laundry room?

☐ Patio or balcony?   ☐ Pets allowed?

Using the Checklist

Make copies of your checklist. Then fill one out each time you call to ask about an apartment. Go through the checklist to make sure you ask all the necessary questions. Be sure to find out about required deposits.

Then, based on what you find out, decide whether to take the next step and visit the apartment. If you decide to visit, take your checklist with you, and double-check all the information.

Lease

A contract for renting a piece of property, such as an apartment. A lease usually states the cost of renting plus other terms, such as the time period.

Deposit

A payment made to hold or reserve something. Also a payment made to cover possible costs.

[FACT]

Finding an Apartment You Can Afford

- **Cost:** How much rent can you afford? Also add up the costs of the utilities you'll have to pay: electricity, heat, and so on. One basic rule is to pay no more than one-third (33%) of your take-home monthly income.

- **Space:** Generally, the bigger the apartment, the higher the rent. Do you need one bedroom or two? If you plan to live by yourself, look into a one-room apartment. It's sometimes called a *studio* or *efficiency apartment.*

- **Location:** Consider the distances from work and school. Housing is usually cheaper the further it is from the city center. But what will this cost you in transportation? And is the area safe?

- **Luxuries:** Do you need a fitness center? A garage? A balcony? You'll pay more for these and other luxuries.

Ways to Lower Your Rent

- **Move-in specials:** Be sure to ask whether any specials are available for new renters. In some cases, the first two months are free if you sign a year's lease. Or the rent might be reduced for the first year if you agree to rent for several years.

- **Caretaking and chores:** Some apartment buildings have a *caretaker:* someone who lives in the building and does maintenance and repairs. Look into being a caretaker. Or ask if you can do any chores in exchange for lower rent. For instance, maybe you can mow the lawn or vacuum the halls.

Tips for Visiting an Apartment

Always visit an apartment before agreeing to rent it. In fact, visit it more than once, if possible: on a weekday, at night, and on a weekend. You don't have to go into the apartment each time. But check out the neighborhood and the apartment's parking lot or street. Also contact the local police department to ask about crime in the area.

When you visit, think about these questions:

- Do you feel safe in the apartment? In the building? In the neighborhood?

- How well are the apartment and the building kept up? Do you see things in need of repair?

- How well is the neighborhood kept up? Are the other houses, apartments, and office buildings in need of repair?

- How do you feel about the landlord? Do you feel you can trust him or her?

- What do you notice about the other renters? Are people in the yard? In the halls? In the parking lot or garage?

- How much noise is there? In the building? Outside the building?

- At night, how well lit is the parking lot or garage? The entryways? The hallways?

Chapter 2

Comparing Classified Rental Ads

Looking at Ads

Dante is trying to find an apartment. He's looked at **classified** ads in the newspaper and online. Here are some examples of the ads he's found:

> **Classified**
>
> Organized or divided into types or groups. *Classified ads* are divided into types, such as apartments for rent, houses for sale, and roommates wanted.

AD 1	AD 3
Charming studio apt, w/w, all elec kit, $650, first and last + $325 sec dep. 555-6329 after 5:00.	2 BR, 2 BA condo, hardwood floors, AC, w/d in unit, pool, avail Aug. 1, $950 + $600 sec dep. Call Jerry 555-3082.
AD 2	AD 4
Furn 1 BR, 1 BA apt., w/w, 1-year lease, $700 first and last + $500 sec dep. Quiet bldg nr river. Avail now. 555-4199.	Efficiency apt sublease June-Sept. w/w, w/d in bldg, pool, exercise room, $500 + $200 sec dep, util inc. Sherry 555-8972

Making Sense of Ads

Abbreviations Used in Housing Ads

To understand these ads, Dante must be able to **interpret** the **abbreviations** they use. Here are some of the abbreviations commonly used in classified ads for housing:

AC	air conditioner	**furn**	furnished
appl	appliances (such as a stove and refrigerator)	**incl**	includes
		kit	kitchen
apt	apartment	**LR**	living room
avail	available (date the apartment will be ready to rent)	**nr**	near
		sec dep	security deposit (also called *damage deposit*)
BA	bathroom		
bldg	building	**unfurn**	unfurnished
BR	bedroom	**w/d**	washer and dryer
elec	electricity, electrical	**w/w**	wall-to-wall carpeting

Interpret	**Abbreviation**
To understand or find the meaning of.	A shortened form of a word.

Terms to Know

Dante also needs to now the meanings of these terms:

condo: a condominium; an apartment unit owned by an individual.

efficiency apartment: a furnished, one-room apartment.

first and last: the first and last months' rent; this money is sometimes paid by the renter as an additional type of deposit.

landlord: the person who owns or manages the apartment.

lease: a written agreement between a landlord and a renter.

notice: an announcement of ending a rental agreement; in many cases, 30 days' notice is required.

security or damage deposit: the money the renter gives the landlord to pay for any damage the renter might do. It's returned if the apartment is left undamaged and clean.

studio apartment: an apartment with one large room and a private bathroom.

sublease: to take on the responsibilities of someone else's lease.

tenant: the person renting the apartment.

Lease Agreements

To rent an apartment, you may have to sign a lease. What are the pros and cons of having a lease?

PROS

- Your rent will stay the same for the lease period (often, one year).

- The rent is usually lower than the rent for an apartment without a lease.

- The landlord can't ask you to leave before the lease is up (unless you break the rules).

- If you agree to rent for several years, the rent might be less than usual or stay the same for the whole time.

CONS

- You must stay until the lease is up or find someone to take over the lease (sublease).

- You can't ask for a reduction in your rent or other changes in terms.

- To stay in the apartment after the end of the lease, you must renew the lease.

Month-to-Month Rental Agreements

Some apartments are rented month to month and don't require a lease. What are the pros and cons of this kind of arrangement?

PROS

- You can move out at the end of the month (after giving 30 days' notice).

- The rental agreement keeps going until you or the landlord gives 30 days' notice to end it.

- You're not committed to stay for a year or more. This is good for students and people with work situations that change.

CONS

- The rent is usually higher for this kind of apartment than one with a lease.

- The landlord can raise the rent at any time.

- The landlord can ask you to move out at the end of the month (with 30 days' notice).

Other Fees Paid by Renters

TYPE OF FEE	PURPOSE?	COST?	REFUNDABLE?
Application fee	Landlord uses it to check your background and credit history	Varies	Usually no
Security or damage deposit	Covers cost of repairs, cleaning, and other problems beyond normal use	Usually equal to one month's rent	Yes, when you move out (unless you owe rent, cause damage, or leave a mess)
Pet fee	Covers damages caused by pets	Varies. Can be a one-time fee (up to hundreds of dollars) or extra rent	Usually yes, if a one-time fee Usually no, if extra rent
Late fee	Charge added onto a late rent payment	Varies. Can be up to $50 for each day the rent is past due	No
Other	Parking Key and lock replacement Rule breaking	Varies	No

CHAPTER **3**

Filling Out a Rental Application

Imagine that you've just found an apartment you really like. And the landlord gives you a rental application to fill out.

What does the landlord want to know? What information should you be expected to provide? What can you expect the landlord to do with this information?

Know What to Expect

Look over the rental application on page 51. It
contains the information a landlord usually asks for
in deciding whether to rent an apartment to someone.

Note that the information includes where you've
lived and where you work. It also includes *credit
references,* which are people and companies with whom
you've done business. You should choose references that
will give a positive report about your bill paying and other
financial responsibilities.

You should expect the landlord to check up on this
information. Also expect the landlord to check your *credit history,*
which is a report about your bill paying and level of debt.

Tips for Filling Out a Rental Application

→ If you have to provide a damage or security
   deposit, pay it with a check rather than
   cash. Also ask for a receipt that says
   what the deposit is for.

→ Check the laws in your state about what kinds of deposits
   a landlord can require. For instance, if you live in California,
   check State Civil Code Section 1950.5, which covers deposits and
   their uses.

→ Get in writing the name and phone number of any landlord you
   leave paperwork and/or a deposit with. Beware of anyone who
   won't give you this information or refuses to provide a receipt.

→ Before you move in, do what's called a *walk-through* of the apartment. Check the condition of the apartment, and make note or take pictures of any damage. Give a copy of the list to the landlord, and keep one for yourself. Refer to this list when you move out. You shouldn't be charged for damage that was already there when you moved in.

Occupant
A renter or lodger.

Authorization
Official approval or permission.

Verify
To prove the accuracy or truth of something.

[FACT]

Who Signs a Lease or Rental Agreement?

- **You:** Before you sign any agreement, make sure you understand and agree to every detail. Keep a signed copy of the lease with your records.

- **Your roommates:** All the people renting the apartment should be on the lease and sign it. This protects all of you if one roommate fails to pay his or her share. If you get a new roommate, ask for a new agreement.

- **Your landlord:** Signing the agreement will help make sure the landlord keeps his or her word to you.

- **Sometimes, a co-signer:** You might be required to have a *co-signer* if you're under 21 or don't have a credit history. A co-signer is someone who agrees to be financially responsible if you fail to pay the rent or other fees.

RENTAL APPLICATION

Property Address _____ Apt. # _____

Monthly Rent $_____Security Deposit $_____Proposed Date of Occupancy____

Name(s) of Applicant(s) _____

Names of Other Occupants _____

Are any of the above under 18? Y / N   Pets? Y / N   Type? _____

Rental History

Present Address_____

For how long? _____ Reason for leaving _____

Name and address of owner or agent _____

Last Previous Address _____   _____

For how long? _____ Reason for leaving _____

Name and address of owner or agent _____

Employment

Present Employer _____ For how long? _____

Address _____ Phone _____

Position _____ Salary $ _____ per _____

Credit References

(1) _____

Address _____ Phone _____

(2) _____

Address _____ Phone _____

Vehicle

Vehicle License Plate # _____ State of registration _____

Make _____ Model _____ Year _____ Color _____

In Case of Emergency

Name of Closest Relative _____ Relationship _____

Address _____ Phone _____

Authorization to Verify Information

I authorize owner/agent to verify the above information, including, but not limited to, obtaining a credit report.

Applicant_____ Phone _____ Date_____

Your Credit Rating

When you get a loan or buy something on credit, your payment activities are reported to credit reporting agencies. These agencies are companies that collect information about your bill paying and borrowing history.

Then, the agencies provide that information to lenders, landlords, employers, and others. They look at the information to see if you are responsible with money. Your credit rating is like your financial "report card."

Having a poor credit rating may keep you from getting a loan, a job, and even a place to live. That's why it's important to pay your bills on time and not take on too much debt.

Tips for Avoiding Rental Scams

Be on the lookout for rental *scams,* in which someone tries to cheat you. Protect yourself by following these tips:

- Question anything that sounds too good to be true.

- Avoid dealing with people who say they live overseas. Ask to deal with a local contact.

- Check with your county government to see who owns the building.

- Ask for a rental application. If the landlord won't provide one, walk away.

- Search ads in local sources, not national ones.

- Use a company that helps people find apartments.

- Talk to renters, neighbors, and the building manager. What do they know about the landlord and the property?

- Don't look at an apartment alone. Always take someone with you.

- Don't pay for anything with cash. Pay with a check instead.

- Don't provide your Social Security number to anyone you don't trust.

Rules for Roommates

Pros and Cons of Having Roommates

Having your own apartment has some *definite* advantages. If you live alone, you can decorate the place as you like. Also, you won't have to put up with the *petty* problems that roommates sometimes cause.

Definite
Clear or obvious.

Petty
Small or unimportant.

But there are also some drawbacks to living alone. It's quite expensive to have your own place. You'll save a lot of money by sharing expenses. Also, a roommate provides instant company. And he or she can introduce you to new people. This will **automatically** increase the number of people in your social circle.

Of course, there are some negatives to having a roommate. For one thing, you'll lose some of your privacy. Another issue is that you may not always get along.

Automatically
Happening without planning or action.

"House Rules"

To prevent having big problems with roommates, consider creating a list of "house rules." It should include basic rules to live by on a day-to-day basis. And everyone in the house should agree to follow them.

Look at the following set of rules that two roommates put together. Check off each rule that seems important to you.

"HOUSE RULES"

☐ Pay your share of the rent five days before the first of the month.

☐ Pay your share of the utilities and other shared bills a week before their due dates.

☐ Buy your own groceries.

☐ Keep your food and beverages in your own area of the refrigerator and on your own shelf in the cupboard.

☐ Put your dishes in the dishwasher after each meal or snack.

☐ Clean up the stove and counter after cooking.

☐ Keep common areas neat.

☐ Wipe down the shower walls and shower door after each shower.

☐ No overnight guests more than three nights a week.

☐ Do your fair share of chores. See the list posted on the refrigerator.

☐ No loud noise after 10:30 p.m.

☐ No loud noise before 7:00 a.m.

☐ No smoking allowed in the apartment.

☐ The person with the master bedroom pays 60% of the rent.

☐ The occupant of the master suite will change every six months.

Choosing a Roommate

Remember: Liking someone doesn't mean you'll be able to stand living together! To choose a roommate, first screen people by phone, e-mail, or social-networking profile. Select a few to interview at a coffee shop. Cover these areas:

- **Schedule:** When do you get up? Go to bed? Go to work? Attend school?

- **Housekeeping:** How often do you vacuum? Wash dishes? Clean the bathroom? Pick up clutter? Take out trash?

- **Social life:** Do you stay out late? Have friends over? Have a girlfriend or boyfriend?

- **Experience:** What did you like and dislike about previous roommates? What conflicts did you have? How did you resolve them?

- **Lifestyle:** Do you smoke? Use drugs? Drink alcohol? Party? How often? How much? Where? Do you have overnight guests? How often?

Expense Agreements

Before selecting roommates, carefully check their references and financial history. Also discuss how to divide expenses before signing a lease. Write up an expense agreement that includes these topics:

- **Rent:** Some landlords require that payment be made in one check. One roommate should write this check, and the other roommates should pay him or her their shares.

- **Utilities:** Decide on a system for payment. Split them evenly? Alternate payments by month? Have different utilities billed to different roommates?

- **Furniture:** Agree on who will provide what. Also agree on how the cost of anything that's purchased will be divided.

- **Food and supplies:** Will all the roommates buy their own? Will they collect money in a fund? Will they share some things but not others? Decide on a system and follow it.

Ways to Handle Disagreements

- **Split the apartment into zones:** Identify shared areas, where you need to compromise and respect each other's preferences. Bedrooms are private. You can keep your room neat or messy. Decorate it however you like. Listen to your favorite music or TV shows—but not too loud.

- **Divide chores:** Match chores to your strengths and interests. Does one of you hate cleaning? Does the other hate cooking or grocery shopping? Agree to have different responsibilities.

- **Agree to disagree:** Do you clash about beliefs or tastes; religion? politics? decorating? Keep these matters private. Limit what you share with your roommate. And respect your differences.

Moving In and Getting Started

When you think about moving, you probably think about hauling boxes and furniture. But do you think about the planning required? In a well-organized move, the heat, lights, and water work from the minute you walk in the door. And so do the telephone, cable TV, and Internet! In fact, a lot of plans have to be made before moving day arrives. Learn what's needed to move and settle into a new home.

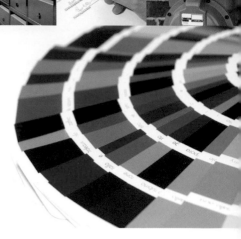

A Few Wrong Moves!

Jaynie and Danielle had been in their new apartment for just over a month. They were pretty well settled in at this point. The apartment was truly beginning to feel like home.

But that wasn't how it felt the day they moved in! The roommates could laugh about it now. But moving day had been something of a disaster.

In the weeks before the move, Jaynie and Danielle planned who would take which bedroom. They also planned how to arrange the furniture in the living room. They even planned what color they'd paint the kitchen. But they didn't make other more important plans for their move.

For example, they didn't plan on renting a truck. Jaynie's boyfriend had a pickup, and her dad had a trailer. Two vehicles seemed like enough. But when the move got underway, both filled up quickly. It took four trips to move Jaynie's belongings and another three to move Danielle's.

Making so many trips took a long time! It was dark before the last box was unloaded. It was also raining. Because neither vehicle was enclosed, many of Danielle's things got wet. She hoped nothing had been ruined.

The roommates also failed to have the electricity turned on. The heat and water came with the apartment. But not the electricity! Danielle called immediately to set up service. She was told it would take several days.

Then, the roommates realized what else they'd forgotten: the telephone, TV, and Internet service. Setting that up would take almost a week.

What a way to start out living in their new apartment! This wasn't at all what Jaynie and Danielle had planned.

CHAPTER **1**

Change of Address Forms

One of the tasks involved in moving is to file a change of address form with the US Postal Service (USPS). Doing so is necessary to have your mail **_forwarded_** to your new address.

In fact, you should file this form with the USPS one to two weeks before you plan to move. It usually takes 7 to 10 business days for the request to go through.

Forwarded
Sent ahead or moved along.

Four Ways to Change Your Address

Online

The USPS encourages people to change their address online, if they can. To do so, go to www.usps.com/umove, and follow the instructions provided.

Here's what you'll be asked to do:

1. Say whether your move is permanent or temporary.

→ Select "Permanent" if you don't plan to move back to this address.

→ Select "Temporary" if you plan to move back within 12 months. In this case, your mail will be forwarded 6 months at a time.

Also provide the date you want mail forwarding to begin.

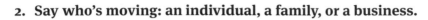

2. **Say who's moving: an individual, a family, or a business.**

→ If it's just you, select "Individual."

→ If it's everyone in your family and you all have the same last name, select "Family."

→ If it's your business, select "Business."

→ If only some members of your family are moving or family members have different last names, each person must do the change of address as an individual. The same goes for roommates. Each person must change his or her address individually.

Also, if you get mail under several different names, you must do a change of address as an individual *for each name.*

Mail Forwarding

One of the services the post office includes with your change of address is mail forwarding. This means the post office will deliver any mail sent to your old address to your new address.

But not all mail is forwarded, and forwarding doesn't last forever. Here's what to expect:

- First-class mail will be forwarded for 12 months.
- Magazines will be forwarded for 60 days.
- Junk mail won't be forwarded, and neither will catalogs.

3. Provide your full name, your old address, your new address, and your e-mail address. Make sure you have all the details of your new address, including the apartment or suite number, and zip code.

Also provide your e-mail address. The USPS will send a *confirmation* of your change of address request.

4. Provide a credit card or debit card number. The USPS charges $1.00 to process a change of address online. So providing payment information is required. The USPS will keep your card information secure to protect you from *fraud*.

For your request to be completed, the billing address for the credit card or debit card must match the address you are moving from *or* the address you are moving to. (If you're moving your business, the billing address must match the address you are moving from.)

Again, the USPS will e-mail you a confirmation of your change of address request. You will receive this confirmation immediately, if your request goes through.

Confirmation
A notice of having received or approved of something.

Fraud
Something that's done to trick or cheat someone out of money or belongings. In most cases, fraud involves a lie or some other kind of dishonesty.

By Telephone

You can also handle a change of address request over the telephone. Call 1-800-ASK-USPS (1-800-275-8777). The same information will be covered as with an online request. And a credit card or debit card will be required, because there is a $1.00 charge.

By Mail

What if you don't want to pay the $1.00 service charge? You can go to the USPS Web site and print out the form: PS 3575. Then, fill it out and mail it to your *current* post office.

In Person

You can also fill out the change of address form and give it to a worker at the post office. You can get form PS 3575 online, from your mail carrier, or at the post office.

[FACT]

Confirmation of Your Change of Address Request

The USPS will confirm your request for a change of address up to four times:

1. By e-mail immediately, if you make the request online
2. In a letter sent to your old address, if you're still living there
3. In a letter sent to your new address
4. With a Welcome Kit that contains helpful information for people new to the area, including coupons and special offers

You should receive the confirmation letter and Welcome Kit at your new address 7 to 10 business days after making the change request. If you don't and you haven't received any forwarded mail, call Customer Service at 1-800-ASK-USPS (1-800-275-8777).

Telling Others of Your Change of Address

Share your new address with anyone who sends you mail that you want to continue to receive. Here's how to go about it:

1. Make a list of companies and organizations you get mail from:
    *   Banks and credit card companies
    *   Utilities (electricity, heat, water, phone)
    *   Insurance companies (auto, health)
    *   Magazine subscriptions
    *   Department of motor vehicles (for driver's license change)
    *   Employer
    *   School

2. Contact each company or organization online, by telephone, or by mail. Many utility companies and credit card companies have their own systems for changing your mailing address. Follow their instructions. Do the same for magazine subscriptions.

3. Keep track of whom you've notified.

4. As you receive forwarded mail, check whether you have notified the company or organization about your address change. If not, do so, and add them to the list of those you have contacted.

CHAPTER **2**

Ordering Phone, Utilities, and Internet Services

Chris had been packing boxes for a week. He'd carefully wrapped all of his *fragile* objects. He'd used enough paper to make sure they wouldn't get broken in the move. And he'd thrown out or given away all the things he'd never use again.

Fragile
Easily broken.

Chris asked a few friends to help him load the boxes and furniture into the van he'd rented. They also said they'd help him unload the van and carry everything into the new apartment.

Chris was excited about moving out on his own. But about a week before the move, his friend Jesse began asking him some questions.

"Did you arrange to get your phone hooked up?" asked Jesse. "Did you call the gas company? What about the electric company? What about water service, or is the landlord taking care of that? Do you need to set up an Internet connection?"

Setting Up New Service

Chris hadn't even thought of all these details! Jesse handed him a list of things to do. He'd found it in a "Mover's Guide" online.

Here's what the list said:

Mover's Guide

✔ If you have a landline, call your local telephone company at least a week before you move. Ask for a new phone number or a change of location for your current phone number. Also have service turned off at your old address the day after you move out.

✔ If you have long-distance telephone service, call the company. Tell them about your move. Doing so will **ensure** your long-distance calling and other services are not interrupted.

✔ Have the gas, electric, and water service connected the day before you move in. Have these services turned off at your old address the day after you move out.

✔ Arrange for cable TV and Internet *installation* at your new address. Check with your cable company. It may offer "bundled" services, including telephone, TV, and Internet. Paying for these services together is often less expensive than paying for them separately.

Chris was grateful for the reminder and for the directions. Of course, he wouldn't have the utilities turned off at his old address. His parents and siblings were still living there! Also, he wouldn't need to do anything about the water service. The landlord at the apartment paid for it, along with the trash and recycling.

Chris wasn't in a hurry to get long-distance service set up, either. He planned to use his cell phone for long-distance calls. But he also made a lot of local calls. So he decided to get a landline for local phone service. And he was eager to get his computer hooked up to the Internet as soon as possible.

Ensure

To make certain.

Installation

The act of setting up or making ready for use.

Tips for Setting Up Utilities

- Ask your landlord which utilities you're responsible for. Also ask for a list of companies to call to set up these different utilities.

- Contact each utility company at least a week before you move. Set up service to start the day before you move in.

- For new customers, utility companies often charge a connection fee, and they usually require a deposit. The amount of the deposit varies widely. Ask if and how the deposit will be refunded.

- Setting up extra services, like cable TV, will likely involve extra charges if the apartment hasn't had the service before.

- Make sure to ask the average monthly cost of your heating bill, if you pay it separately. In many climates, the bill is higher in winter months.

Pros and Cons of Having Utilities Included in Your Rent

PROS

CONS

- Budgeting is easier. You pay just one bill a month, and it doesn't change from month to month.

- Dividing up expenses with roommates is simple.

- The usual yearly increase in rent is often less than the increase in energy costs.

- You have less control over how much you pay. Cost-saving steps like turning off extra lights won't save you any money.

- You are less likely to try to conserve energy.

- The part of your rent that goes to pay utilities is based on the renters who use the most.

Pros and Cons of Having a Landline

PROS

CONS

PROS

- In a remote area, you'll have more dependable coverage than many cell phones provide.

- A landline won't get lost, stolen, or damaged nearly as often as a cell phone may.

- The phone will work longer than a cell phone without recharging the battery. (Phones with portable handsets require recharging but not as often as cell phones.)

CONS

- You'll get more calls from people selling things or taking surveys.

- You won't have features such as text messaging, games, a built-in camera, e-mail, a schedule planner, or Internet connection.

CHAPTER **3**

Buying Essential Household Goods

Furniture

If you're just starting out, you probably don't have much furniture of your own. Even if you have some large pieces, you might decide not to move them. After all, it can be very expensive to move furniture—especially if you're moving far away. Sometimes it makes more sense to sell your old stuff and buy new or used furniture at your new location.

Here are some smart options for *acquiring* furniture:

→ **Check with your relatives.** Family members are often glad to help young people get started. Perhaps your grandparents have an old couch they don't need anymore. Or maybe an aunt and uncle have recently bought new bedroom furniture and are willing to pass along their old pieces.

Acquire
To get or to buy.

Tell your relatives that you're moving into your own place soon. You might be surprised by the help you'll be offered!

→ **Renting or leasing furniture.** If you're not sure how long you'll stay in your new apartment, renting or leasing is a good option. Usually, you'll have to sign a one-year lease. If you rent for a shorter period, the monthly price will be higher.

What's the main advantage of renting or leasing furniture? You'll be able to fill up an entire apartment for little money. But the obvious disadvantage is that even after a year of payments, you won't own anything.

→ **Buying furniture.** You can buy new or used furniture in all price ranges. Check the Salvation Army, Goodwill stores, and St. Vincent de Paul stores for used furniture of acceptable quality. Also check out private secondhand stores, garage and yard sales, auctions, and thrift shops. Another possibility is to look at the classified ads in the newspaper or online.

If you want to buy new furniture, compare prices at discount furniture and department stores. Many furniture stores also have "odds and ends" sections or rooms. You might find a piece that's slightly damaged but sold at a great discount.

→ **Making furniture.** You'd be surprised at how easy it is to make some kinds of furniture. You can make a coffee table, end table, desk, lamp, bookcase, bed, or sofa with a few basic materials and tools. Many books and Web sites are available that show you how to do this.

Other Basic Household Goods

In addition to furniture, you'll need some kitchen utensils and dishes. You'll also need bathroom supplies and linens (sheets and towels). And you'll need small appliances such as a clock radio, iron, vacuum cleaner, toaster, and coffee maker.

As with buying furniture, don't buy household *goods* without carefully comparing prices. You can find low prices at many discount stores.

Goods
Supplies or products.

Tips for Buying a Couch

- **Cost:** A free or cheap used couch can be a great deal, especially if you're just starting out. A midpriced couch costs about $800 and will last five years or so. A high-end couch will cost $800 or more but will last much longer.

- **Type:** Couches come in many styles. A good option for an apartment is one that can double as a guest bed. Look into a futon or sofa sleeper (also called a *pullout couch*).

- **Size:** Choose a size that won't make the room look crowded. Also consider where you will place the couch. Make sure it won't block anything important—like a door. In a small space, a loveseat is a good option. It will also cost less than a full-sized couch. Sectionals are popular but take up a lot of room.

- **Material:** Pick fabric that is sturdy, is easy to clean, and resists stains. Also look into putting slipcovers over fabric that is worn, stained, or unattractive.

Goodwill Stores

Are you looking for bargains on household items? A good place to start is your local Goodwill store.

At a Goodwill store, you'll find all kinds of used household items. The items have been donated to Goodwill and then cleaned or fixed up. And they're sold at bargain prices. At Goodwill Outlet stores, you buy goods by the pound, which is even cheaper.

Goodwill Industries International is a charity. Its goal is to help people in need find opportunities. And helping people reach their goals helps them give back to their communities.

Furniture-Buying Basics

- **Start with the five basic pieces:** They include a bed, a table for eating, dining chairs, a couch, and a dresser. You'll use these pieces no matter where you live. If you can, buy quality pieces that will last.

- **Measure before you buy:** Draw a floor plan of the apartment that includes exact measurements. Note the locations of doors and windows. Outside the apartment, measure elevators, stairwells, halls, and doorways. Make sure you know how much room you'll have to carry in big pieces of furniture.

- **Arrange the rooms:** Before buying, plan what can go where and how big a new piece can be. Make cutouts of furniture from newspaper or cardboard to use in planning. Also make use of online tools (such as www.bhg.com/decorating/arrange-a-room).

[FACT]

Buying a Better Bed

- **Size:** What best fits the space: a twin (39" x 75"), a full (54" x 75"), a queen (60" x 80"), or a king (76" x 80")? Note that an extra-deep or extra-long mattress will require special-sized bedding.

- **Mattress:** Try different styles in stores. Test the level of firmness, and check out the type of material. A firm mattress is good for back and stomach sleepers. A soft mattress is good for side sleepers. Material choices include an innerspring mattress and box spring, memory foam, or an air mattress.

- **Bed frame:** A solid steel frame with large, heavyweight castors (wheels) is a good choice. It will last through several mattresses. Some bed frames adjust to fit different-size mattresses.

- **Quality:** A high-quality mattress will last 10 years or more. And a good night's sleep and a healthy back are worth a lot, too.

Renting a Moving Truck

If you work for a big company that will pay for your move, you're very lucky! In that case, you can hire movers. They will even pack your boxes for you.

But if you're like most people, you'll have to pack your own boxes and pay for your own move. So, you'll probably have to rent a moving truck or a trailer.

Renting a Trailer

If you have only a few boxes and pieces of furniture, a trailer will likely be big enough. Check what sizes of trailers are available. Also try to get an enclosed trailer, rather than an open trailer.

In addition, make sure the trailer hitch will fit on the back of the car or truck you plan to use. And be sure the car or truck has enough power to pull a trailer without being damaged. The rental company will be able to provide you with this information.

Renting a Truck

If you need to rent a truck, you should know these things:

→ You have many options in terms of size and cost. The size of the truck determines the price. Don't rent a bigger truck than you need.

→ For a one-bedroom apartment, a 14-foot truck should be big enough. For a two-bedroom apartment, you'll probably need a 17-foot truck.

- → Some companies charge a set rental fee, and you pay for the gas. Other companies charge *mileage* and a fee, and they *refund* your gas expenses.

- → You'll probably need a credit card or debit card to reserve the truck and to pick it up. A deposit might be charged and then refunded if you return the truck in good shape.

- → The rental agency will need to know your age. Some companies won't rent a truck to anyone under 18.

- → Before you sign a rental contract, you'll have to show a *valid* driver's license.

- → You'll also need insurance on the rental truck. You may be covered by your own personal auto insurance. Some policies cover you for a rental, including a rental truck. If so, you won't have to buy more insurance from the rental company. Check with your insurance company to see if you're already covered.

Mileage
The distance traveled in miles.

Refund
To return a payment that's been made.

Valid
Proven to be legal or correct.

Packing Tips

- Get free boxes from grocery, liquor, and shipping stores. Or buy boxes from a moving or truck rental company.

- Wrap fragile items in newspaper, T-shirts, towels, or blankets. Clearly mark boxes containing these items "Fragile!"

- Cover furniture with sheets, blankets, or rugs. Protect wood or metal ends from being scraped or bent.

- Pack similar items together.

- Pack heavy items in small boxes and light items in larger boxes.

- Label all the boxes. List their contents or the rooms they'll go in.

- Set aside a box of cleaning supplies for moving day. Don't pack or move these supplies!

- Pack a suitcase of personal items you'll need the first few days after your move.

- Load the truck with the heaviest items first. Balance the weight from side to side. And tie down items that might shift or fall over in the move.

Reserve a Vehicle in Advance

At most rental businesses, the trailers and trucks are reserved several weeks in advance. In a college community, this is especially true at the beginnings and ends of semesters.

Be sure to make a reservation early. If you wait too long, you might not be able to get the vehicle you need.

Are You Old Enough to Rent a Truck?

Age requirements vary by company. Ask each company you talk to about renting. Some will rent to anyone 18 or older with a valid driver's license. Others require you to be at least 24 years old. Most companies with older age requirements make some exceptions. Be sure to ask.

To make a reservation, you will probably need a credit card or debit card. Nothing will be charged on the card until you pick up the vehicle. But you might get charged a fee if you don't pick up a vehicle you've reserved. Cancel the reservation if you change your mind about renting the vehicle.

Timetable for Moving

TIME FRAME	TASK
4–6 weeks ahead	• Plan a budget for moving expenses. • Decide what belongings you'll move.
2–4 weeks ahead	• Research truck and trailer rentals, and make a reservation. • Get boxes and packing tape. • Begin packing. Start with items you don't need to use. • Ask friends and family for help on moving day.
1–7 days ahead	• Check with your landlord: Do you need to reserve a parking space or an elevator on move-in day? • Confirm the truck or trailer rental and what helpers you'll have. • Pack and label everything.
Moving day	• Pick up the rental truck or trailer. • Put fragile items and things you'll need the first few days in your car. • Load the truck or trailer. Move. Unload. • Provide water and food for your helpers.

Solving Common Problems

No matter how carefully you plan, you'll still have problems from time to time. Maybe you'll have a water leak in your apartment and have trouble getting it fixed. Maybe you'll have a roommate who eats your food and doesn't replace it. Or maybe you'll have an unexpected expense, such as car repairs. Whatever the case, you'll be better able to handle your problems if you know your options in advance.

Reminding Others of the Rules

Marcus was working full time and going to college. Most weeks, he felt like he didn't have a minute to spare. And this week was final exams week, so he was especially busy.

The week had started out badly. Marcus's roommate, T. J., had invited friends over Sunday night. They'd stayed up late and kept Marcus awake, too. And they'd left a mess in the living room: empty pizza boxes and dirty plates and glasses.

When Marcus got up the next morning, he was *not* happy! But he had to get to work. He would have to talk with T. J. later. Apparently, T. J. needed to be reminded of two of their "house rules": No late-night guests on school nights. And clean up after yourself and your friends.

Marcus was tired all day Monday, but he made it through work. That night, he studied for the final exam he had on Tuesday. T. J. was at work, so the apartment was quiet. It seemed cold, too, Marcus thought.

He turned up the dial to make the heat come

on, but nothing happened. Great! The heat wasn't working. This had happened twice before. And the apartment owner had been slow to fix the problem. Marcus called the owner right away and left a voice-mail message. "The problem needs to be fixed immediately!" he said.

Marcus also planned on talking to someone at the state government. The apartment owner had a legal responsibility to provide heat. Marcus didn't want to overreact. He just wanted the problem fixed so it wouldn't happen again.

The last thing he needed right now was to get sick. Paying medical bills wasn't in the budget.

CHAPTER 1

Do's and Don'ts for Tenants

Kenji has just moved. He's the **tenant** of a condo on the second floor of a large building. It has a nice deck overlooking the pool area. It also has a fairly big storage area right off the deck. And it even has a fireplace!

Tenant

Someone who rents an apartment, home, or other property.

What You May Want to Do

Kenji has a one-year lease, and he's looking forward to settling in. Here's what he plans to do as soon as he gets unpacked:

→ Plant tomatoes and flowering vines in pots and put them on the deck. He'll train the vines to grow around the deck railing and up the walls on the sides of the deck.

→ Install a state-of-the-art sound system, so he can really enjoy his music and TV. He'll put some speakers outside on the deck, too.

→ Get a large hamper with a cloth bag liner. That way, he can carry all of his laundry to the laundry room at once. He plans to leave the laundry there until all his loads are done. Because the dryers are so expensive, he'll dry towels outside on the deck.

→ Buy a cord of wood, and store it on the deck. It will be handy there, and he won't have to keep buying wood for the fireplace.

→ Paint the bedroom walls red and get a black bedspread.

What Your Lease Says You Can Do

Kenji is going to have a few disappointments! The lease he signed includes the following rules for tenants:

→ All *exterior* areas that are open to public view must be kept neat. Nothing shall be stored on the tiled areas outside individual front doors. Items allowed on decks are limited to patio furniture and potted plants.

Common Problems Tenants Have with Landlords

- **Not making repairs:** A landlord generally has 7 to 14 days after being told of a problem to make the repair. An emergency problem must be fixed within 2 days.

- **Overcharging late fees:** A landlord can charge a late fee of up to 10% of the rent. Anything higher is considered unfair and should be questioned.

- **Entering the rental without permission:** A landlord must give a tenant 12 to 24 hours' notice before entering the rental for any reason.

- **Keeping security or damage deposits:** Some landlords don't return some or all of the deposit when a tenant moves out, and they don't tell the tenant why. The landlord is required to send a letter explaining why the deposit isn't being refunded. The landlord must also list the costs of any cleaning and repairs.

- **Residents** shall not allow climbing or clinging plants to grow up the walls of the building or on deck railings. Except for ground-floor units, no planter or other container may be set on the railing of a deck. All planters, inside and out, must have a pan or other container to stop water runoff.

- No exterior clotheslines shall be installed or maintained. There shall be no outside drying of clothes, carpets, or the like on any unit or in the common areas.

- Laundry rooms are to be kept free of litter. Clothes must be removed promptly from machines.

- No loud music or other noises that could disturb other tenants is permitted.

- Any permanent improvement to the interior must be approved by the owner in advance. This includes painting and wallpapering.

Look back over Kenji's "wish list." How many of those things will he *not* be able to do?

Exterior
Outside.

Resident
Someone who lives in a particular place. Someone can be a resident of an apartment or even a city or state.

Safety Tips for Tenants

- Keep your doors and windows locked, whether you're home or away.

- Don't let people who aren't tenants into the building. And if you see a stranger enter the building, call 911.

- When someone knocks at your door, always ask who it is. Keep the door locked unless you're sure you can trust the person.

- Don't let strangers into your apartment. Have repair people show their company ID cards.

- Keep valuable items out of sight. Lock up your laptop computer even when you're home.

- If you own a bike, keep it locked.

- Ensure that smoke detectors are working. Test the batteries monthly.

- Contact your landlord if you have any concerns about security.

Common Problems Landlords Have with Tenants

- **Paying rent late:** Rent is considered late if the full amount isn't paid by the due date. The landlord can charge a late fee, if it's stated in the lease.

- **Not paying the last month's rent:** Some tenants think the security or damage deposit covers the last rent payment before they move out. In fact, the deposit is intended to cover cleaning and repair expenses after the tenants have moved out. When tenants leave the space in good condition, they get back their deposit.

- **Behaving badly:** Examples of bad behavior include loud parties, loud music, violence, wild physical activity, rude conduct, and damaging the property.

- **Breaking rules:** The rules tenants are expected to follow are provided In the lease or rental agreement. Any penalties are stated, as well.

CHAPTER 2

Unexpected Expenses: Revising Your Budget

Have you ever heard the saying "Expect the unexpected"? This is certainly good advice when it comes to your budget.

Suppose you create a budget, and it looks as if it will work. You go along for six months, and you have enough money to cover all your expenses.

Then an unexpected problem comes along! Maybe something major goes wrong with your car. Maybe your dentist says you need a root canal. Or perhaps your computer crashes.

Whatever it is, you haven't planned for it. And since you're determined not to touch your savings, what can you do?

You'll need to *revise* your budget.

Building an Emergency Fund

Financial advisors recommend having an emergency fund. You should save enough money to cover at least three to six months' worth of expenses.

How can you build your emergency fund?

1. **Start small.** Save $10 a week, just to get started. Look at your budget, and decide where you can cut expenses. Over time, gradually increase how much you save every month.

2. **Set a goal.** If saving three months' expenses sounds like too much, try saving $1,000. When you reach that goal, increase it.

3. **Open an account.** Set up an emergency savings account. Keep this money separate from your regular savings and checking accounts. And use this money only in true emergencies.

Revising Jake's Budget

Jake has a monthly income of $2,000 a month. His monthly expenses are listed in the following chart. Find all the *variable* expenses listed:

Variable

Able to change.

MONTHLY EXPENSES	
Rent	$500
Utilities (gas, electricity, water, garbage)	$100
Phone	$55
Cable TV and Internet	$80
Transportation (car payment, gas, oil, parking)	$300
Savings	$100
Insurance (health, renter's, car)	$200
Charities	$20
Credit card payments	$120
Medical/dental (drugs and treatment not covered by insurance)	$50
Household maintenance (cleaning products, repairs)	$30
Food (groceries, nonfood items in grocery bill, restaurants, take-out)	$260
Personal maintenance (clothing, laundry, haircuts health and grooming products)	$50
Movie subscription service	$15
Recreation	$120

Now, imagine that Jake has some car trouble. He needs the car to get to work, so he can't put off fixing it.

The repairs will cost $628. Jake decides to put the charge on a credit card and pay it off within six months. Including interest, he figures it will cost him $672, or $112 a month.

Where will Jake get this $112 a month?

→ He decides to reduce his savings to $75 a month for a while.

→ He thinks he can save another $30 a month by going out to eat less and taking his lunch to work more often.

→ By **conserving** energy at home, he hopes to save some money on utilities.

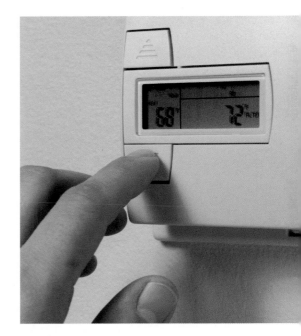

→ He thinks he can trim a few dollars off his recreation spending.

→ Finally, he can reduce his movie subscription service or even cancel it for a few months. Right now, it's a luxury he can't afford.

You can use the same method to reduce your expenses when you have unexpected bills. Revising your budget as needed will help you avoid going deeply in debt.

Conserve
To use carefully and not waste.

Renter's Insurance

Another option is to purchase renter's insurance. This kind of insurance covers unexpected expenses, such as replacing the contents of your apartment in case of a fire or a break-in.

Typically, renter's insurance costs from $150 to $400 a year. It's an added expense but less costly than replacing all your valuables.

Avoid the Credit Card Trap

Going into debt is a lot easier than getting out of debt. And because of the interest and fees charged, using credit cards is a quick way to build debt. Over time, the interest charged can more than double the amount of the original purchase. That debt can take years to pay off.

Follow these tips for using a credit card:

- Don't use a credit card to buy something you don't need and don't have the money for.

- Always pay your credit card bill on time. Paying late will result in fees being added. And your credit rating will be damaged.

- As much as possible, pay off your entire bill every month. If you pay only part of the bill, you'll pay interest on the rest.

Renter's Insurance

Landlords are responsible only for damage to the building. Renters are responsible for the following:

1. Damage or loss of their personal property (including theft and disasters such as fire, water leaks, wind, and hail)

2. Medical and legal expenses for personal injuries they cause (accidentally or not)

3. Temporary housing in the case of a disaster

The renter pays a small monthly fee called a *premium*. Then he or she will be covered for all three kinds of risks. The cost of renter's insurance may depend on where you live and the value of what you own. But shop around to get the best rate. You might get a deal when buying it with your auto insurance. Also ask about price reductions for having deadbolt locks, smoke alarms, and sprinklers and for being a nonsmoker.

CHAPTER **3**

Revising Rules for Roommates

When Gina, Leila, and Kym moved in together, they made up a list of rules. They wanted to ensure their shared bills got paid on time. And they wanted to ensure they'd be respectful and ***considerate*** of one another.

Each young woman has her own copy of these rules:

RULES FOR OUR APARTMENT

- Pay your share of rent on the first of the month. (If you make us have late fees, you'll have to pay them.)
- Pay your share of utility and phone bills on the 15th of the month.
- Don't eat other people's food without permission.
- Label your **staples** in the cabinets. Use only your own!
- Label your foods and beverages, and keep them on your own shelf in the refrigerator.
- Wash your own dishes, and clean up after yourself in kitchen.
- Store personal belongings in your own room.
- Take turns cleaning the bathroom. Every third day is your turn!
- Conserve energy. Turn off lights you're not using. Don't run water needlessly.
- **Secure** all common belongings (such as shared bicycles and scooters) in the locked storage area. Also make sure to close and lock all doors and windows at night or when you leave the apartment.
- No loud music.
- No smoking.

Staples
Basic supplies or ingredients.

Secure
To make safe.

Revising the Rules

Three months went by with
no difficulties. Then, the
roommates started noticing a
problem.

The bread each person
bought on Saturday turned stale
and moldy before it was half gone.
Packages of lunchmeat started to go bad before they were used. When
each person bought a bunch of bananas, they were all rotten within
three days.

The roommates had to throw out milk, eggs, and other foods
because they went bad. And they were wasting staples, too. Crackers
and cereal often got stale soon after being opened.

So, the roommates decided to have a meeting and revise their rules.

"Here's my idea," Gina said. "Let's make a food budget and share
the cost and the food. That way, we can cut down on the waste. Instead
of buying three loaves of bread all at once, we'll buy one and share it.
Then we'll buy another one. That way, we won't be throwing out stale
bread every few days. Instead of buying three pounds of hamburger,
we'll buy one and share it. The same goes
for all the food we've been wasting.
We can each put the same amount
of money into the pot. Then we can
take turns shopping, using a list.
That makes more sense, don't
you think?"

food
budget

"That will work for us," Kym said, "since we all eat pretty much the same things and the same amounts. Each of us spends about the same amount on food, don't we? So, this new system sounds good. Let's try it and see how it goes."

"Good idea," said Leila. "If it doesn't seem to work, we can always have another meeting. We might have to revise the rules a few times before we figure things out once and for all."

Staying on Top of Bills

- Keep a whiteboard or bulletin board in a common area. List utilities and rent. Note who owes what and when it's due. Have each person check off when his or her payment has been made. Everyone will know who's behind in paying.

- Put each utility in one roommate's name. Decide whose name will be on which bill. Collect the money for and pay your bill on time. This will help you protect your credit rating.

- Read your lease! Remember that each person who signed it is legally responsible for the full rent.

- If all or any part of the rent is late, the landlord can charge a fee. Also, not paying the full rent can mean being *evicted*, or getting kicked out.

Communication Guidelines for Roommates

Living with roommates requires give and take. Keep these guidelines in mind for effective communication:

- Deal with problems as they happen. Don't let things build up.
- Be specific in explaining problems. Say what's on your mind.
- Be respectful and stay calm. Getting emotional will create bad feelings and delay solving the problem.
- Listen. Don't assume you know others' reasons or opinions.
- Avoid blaming. Focus on fixing the problem, not who or what caused it.
- Suggest solutions when possible. Offer to compromise.

[FACT]

How Long Does Food Stay Fresh?

For food that's been opened and is in the refrigerator, follow these guidelines:

Pasta sauce:	5 days
Mayonnaise:	2 months
Hard cheese:	3–4 weeks
Soft cheese:	1–2 weeks
Eggs:	3–5 weeks
Leftovers:	3–4 days
Apples:	3–6 months
Cold cuts/Lunch meat:	3–5 days
Delivery pizza:	3–4 days
Ketchup, oil, salad dressing:	See the package for the expiration date
Milk:	See the package for the expiration date

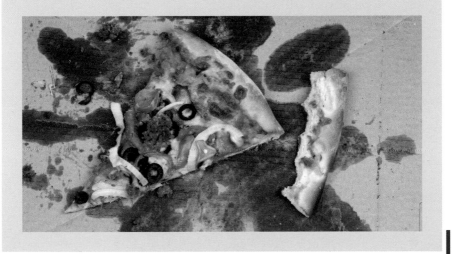

CHAPTER 4

Tenants' Legal Rights

What Are Tenants' Rights?

It was February, and the weather was very cold. Casey noticed a serious problem in the apartment he was renting. The heater didn't work.

Casey called his landlord and left a voice-mail message about the broken heater. By the end of the following day, the landlord still had not fixed the problem or returned Casey's call.

Next, Casey wrote a letter to the landlord. A week passed. Still, Casey heard nothing.

That's when Casey decided to get the heater fixed on his own. He would deduct the cost of the repairs, subtracting it from his next rent payment.

Is Casey allowed to do this? The answer is "yes." In fact, he could have had the repairs made after only a few days, because the weather was so cold. Like all tenants, Casey has certain rights.

What Are Landlords' Responsibilities?

Landlords have legal responsibilities to their tenants. Read the following list of landlords' responsibilities in Casey's state. The laws in other states may differ. If you rent an apartment, condo, or house, you should find out about such laws in your own state.

A LANDLORD MUST:

1. Correct **violations** of health or housing codes that **endanger** tenants' health or safety.

2. Keep common areas **reasonably** clean and safe from defects that could cause fires or other accidents.

3. Provide a smoke detector.

4. Make sure the rental property is not infested with rodents, insects, or other pests when the tenant moves in. Control pests during the tenancy, except in the case of a single-family residence.

5. Keep the rental in as good repair as it was or should have been at the beginning of tenancy. Normal wear and tear is acceptable.

6. Provide **adequate** locks and keys.

7. Keep electrical, plumbing, and heating systems in good repair. Repair any appliances or other facilities that are supplied for renters' use.

8. Keep the rental unit weather tight.

9. Provide garbage cans. Arrange for trash removal for tenants, except for those who occupy single-family residences.

10. Provide access to a reasonable amount of heat, as well as hot and cold water.

Violations
Cases of breaking the rules or the law.

Reasonably
According to common sense.

Endanger
To put at risk.

Adequate
Enough or proper.

Avoiding Legal Troubles with Landlords

- Know your legal rights and responsibilities.
- Understand the details of your lease or rental agreement.
- Discuss problems with your landlord. Try to solve them early on.
- Keep written records of problems and communications. Include dates.
- Ask for repairs in writing.
- If your landlord ignores your concerns, show him or her your records. Remind the landlord of his or her responsibilities.

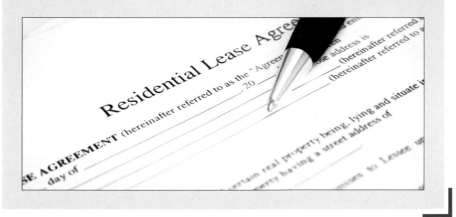

Getting Back Your Security or Damage Deposit

1. **Move-in inspection:** Examine floor, walls, and ceilings. Check the carpet. Test appliances, lights, water pressure, and sink drainage. Note wear and tear and damaged items.

2. **Record:** During your inspection, write down details. Take photos and date them. Do this with your landlord, or have someone with you. Each of you should sign and date the paper. Keep a copy, and give one to your landlord.

3. **Re-inspect:** When you move out, recheck everything you checked in your move-in inspection.

4. **Deductions:** Your landlord will charge you for repairs if you've caused new damage. Your landlord will also charge you for cleaning if you leave behind a mess. You can't be charged for normal wear and tear.

5. **Deadline:** Your landlord usually has 14 to 30 days to return your full deposit or a statement about how it was spent. Otherwise, you can sue him or her.

Word List

abbreviation	chores	definite	essential
ability	classified	delay	estimate
access	co-worker	delicate	examine
accuracy	college	dependence	expectation
acquire	committed	deposit	expensive
activity	communicate	details	express
adequate	competency	determine	exterior
adjust	complex	development	
admit	compliment	difficulty	fee
advance	compromise	disagreement	focus
agreement	condition	disaster	fragile
apologize	confidence	discount	fraud
application	confirmation	disturb	fund
appointment	conflict	divide	furnish
assessment	consequence	donate	
assume	conserve	drawbacks	gossip
attitude	consideration		graduate
authority	constructive	eager	guidelines
automatically	contact	earnings	
available	cooperate	effective	household
	credit	efficient	housing
bargain	criticism	emergency	
behavior		employer	ignore
budget	damage	enable	immature
	debit	enclosed	impression
category	debt	encourage	income
charity	decrease	endanger	influence
checklist	deduct	ensure	ingredients

116

Word List

insecurity
inspection
install
insurance
interest
interior
interpret
interview
introduce
inventory
involve

key

landlord
lease
legal
lifestyle
luxury

maintenance
manage
material
maximum
mileage

negative

obvious
occupant
online
option
organization

particular
patience
penalty
percentage
permanent
polite
potential
previous
priorities
privacy
progress

qualities
quantity

readiness
receipt
recharge
recommend
refund
refuse
register

relative
repair
replace
reservation
resident
resist
resolve
respond
responsibility
reveal
revise
risks
roommate

savings
scam
schedule
security
select
signal
similar
situation
solution
source
specific
staples
storage
summarize

temporary
tenant
terms
tips
topic
transportation

uninterrupted
urgent
utilities

valid
values
variable
vary
vehicle
verify
victim
violation

willing

Index

Address, changing of,
  65–69
  confirmation of, 67, 68
  telling others of, 69
  ways of, 65–68
Ads. *See* Classified ads
Apartments, 36–41
  applications for, 48–53
  costs of, 37, 38, 40, 47,
    75. *See also* Deposits;
    Utilities
  features of, 37, 38
  finding/selecting of,
    38–39, 42–44
  landlords of. *See*
    Landlords
  renting of. *See* Leases;
    Rental agreements
  roommates of. *See*
    Roommates
  tenants of. *See* Tenants
  visiting of, 38, 41, 50,
    115
Applications, for
    apartments, 48–53
  example of, 51
  fees for, 47
  information on, 49
  tips for, 49–51
Attitudes, assessment of,
    14–19
  and behaviors, 16–17
  changing of, 18
  effects of, 15, 17, 18

Beds, buying of, 81. *See
    also* Furniture
Budgets/Budgeting, 26–31
  adjusting/revising of,
    30, 98–103
  balancing of, 28
  examples of, 28,
    100–101
  steps in, 26–30
  tools for, 29

Cable TV service, setting
    up of, 72, 73. *See also*
    Utilities
Calendars, 20, 21–23. *See
    also* Time
Caretakers, 40
Cell phones
  vs. landlines, 75. *See
    also* Telephone service
  tools on, 21, 23
Change of address. *See*
    Address
Classified ads, for
    apartments,
    42–44
Computer software, for
    budgeting, 29
Couches, buying of, 79. *See
    also* Furniture
Credit cards, tips for use
    of, 102
Credit history/rating, 49,
    52

Damage deposits. *See*
    Deposits
Debt, avoiding of, 101, 102
Deposits, for apartments
  laws about, 49, 115
  purposes of, 39, 47, 97
  refunding of, 47, 50, 94,
    97, 115

Emergency fund, saving
    for, 99
Expenses, 27–28, 29, 31.
    See also Budgets/
    Budgeting

Food, buying/storing of,
    31, 109
Forwarding, of mail, 65, 66.
    See also Address
Friends, qualities of, 19
Furniture, buying of,
    76–78, 79, 80, 81

Goals, setting/achieving of,
    22, 25
Goodwill stores, 79
Groceries, buying/storing
    of, 31, 109

Household goods, buying
    of, 78, 79. *See also*
    Furniture

Index

Income, 26, 29. *See also* Budgets/Budgeting
Insurance, for renters, 102, 103
Internet service, setting up of, 72, 73. *See also* Utilities

Knowledge and skills, assessment of, 8–13
general types of, 9
specific types of, 19–11

Landlines, 72, 73, 75. *See also* Telephone service
Landlords
problems with, 94, 114
responsibilities of, 110–113. *See also* Leases
trustworthiness of, 41, 49, 50, 53
Late fees, for rent payments, 47, 94, 97, 102, 105, 107
Leases
pros/cons of, 45
signing of, 50, 107
terms of, 38, 50, 94–95, 97, 107, 114

Money, wasting of, 31. *See also* Budgets/ Budgeting

Month-to-month, rental agreements for, 46. *See also* Rental agreements
Move-in inspections, of apartments, 115. *See also* Apartments, visiting of
Moving vehicles, renting of, 82–87
age requirement for, 86
loading of, 85
reserving of, 86, 87
types of, 82–84

Online tools, for budgeting, 29

Packing, before moving, 85, 87
Peer pressure, handling of, 10

Readiness, for independence, 8–9
Rental agreements, 46, 50. *See also* Leases
Rental housing. *See* Apartments
Renters' insurance, 102, 103
Roommates, 54–59
choosing of, 57, 58
communicating with, 108

disagreements with, 55, 59
pros/cons of, 54–55
rules for, 56, 105–107

Scams, and rentals, 53
Schedules, 20, 21–23. *See also* Time
Security deposits. *See* Deposits
Self-confidence, development of, 15
Social skills, development of, 13

Telephone service, setting up of, 72, 73, 75. *See also* Cell phones; Utilities
Tenants, 92–97
plans of, 93
problems with, 97
requirements/ responsibilities of, 94–95, 97. *See also* Leases; Rental agreements
rights of, 110, 114
safety tips for, 96
Time, managing of, 20–25
calendars/schedules for, 20, 21–23
and goal setting/ achieving, 22, 25
"to-do" lists for, 23–24

Index

wasting of, 24
"To-do" lists, 23–24. *See also* Time
Trailers, for moving 82–83. *See also* Moving vehicles
Trucks, for moving, 83–84. *See also* Moving vehicles

TV service, setting up of, 72, 73. *See also* Utilities

Utilities
    costs of, 27, 38, 40, 74, 101
    payments for, 56, 58, 72, 105, 107
    and leases, 71, 73, 74

setting up of, 71, 72–73, 74

Walk-throughs, of apartments, 50. *See also* Apartments, visiting of
Web sites, for budgeting tools, 29
Work, wasting time at, 24